The Developing
Artist

PIANO LITERATURE BOOK 1

ORIGINAL KEYBOARD CLASSICS

REVISED EDITION

Late Elementary

Compiled and edited by

Nancy and Randall Faber

Production Coordinator: Jon Ophoff
Cover: Terpstra Design, San Francisco
Engraving: Dovetree Productions, Inc.

FABER
PIANO ADVENTURES®
3042 Creek Drive
Ann Arbor, Michigan 48108

THE PERIODS OF MUSIC HISTORY

BAROQUE

Dates: 1600–1750, a time of glittering royal courts in Europe, wigs on men, and the colonization of America.

Style: The word "Baroque" describes a very decorative style of art and architecture.

Composers: Bach, Handel, and Telemann are famous Baroque composers. A gavotte by Telemann is included in this collection. Telemann lived in Hamburg, Germany, where he was the town music director.

The Keyboard: The harpsichord, clavichord, and organ were the keyboard instruments used during the Baroque period. The piano was not invented until the early 1700s. (The student may wish to explore playing the Baroque pieces on the harpsichord setting of a digital keyboard.)

CLASSICAL

Dates: Approximately 1750–1830, the time of the French and American Revolutions, Thomas Jefferson, and the rise and fall of Napoleon. Men still wore wigs and lace, bowed politely, and danced the minuet.

Style: The music of the Classical period is generally elegant and melodic. Composers and artists preferred simplicity to the grandeur of the Baroque.

Composers: Mozart, Haydn, and Beethoven were the major composers of the Classical period. This book includes pieces by Haydn (who worked at the splendid palace of Prince Esterhazy) and Diabelli (a friend of Beethoven).

The Keyboard: The early piano was known as the *fortepiano*. It became popular because the performer could play the keys with a loud (*forte*) or soft (*piano*) touch.

ROMANTIC

Dates: Approximately 1830–1910, a time of industrial growth, the Civil War in the United States, and Queen Victoria's reign over the British Empire.

Style: The music of the Romantic period became more emotional and personal. Pieces often expressed an event or story, such as "The Hunt" and "Tarantella" in this collection.

Composers: Featured in this collection are Gurlitt, who taught at the Hamburg Conservatory; Schytte, a Danish pianist who settled in Germany; and Lynes, a prominent composer in Boston who studied at the Leipzig Conservatory.

The Keyboard: The *pianoforte* (now shortened to piano) gained power and size with the use of steel and brass.

CONTEMPORARY

Dates: 1900 to the present, the time of the automobile, the phonograph, sending man to the moon, and the invention of the computer.

Style: Modern music is wide and varied. Characteristics include dissonant harmonies, exciting rhythms, and a wide range of dynamics. "The Busy Machine" and "On the Ocean Floor" are examples of the varied sounds of 20th century music.

Composers: During the 20th century, women composers and American composers began to achieve recognition. It is an exciting time for musicians as today's composers draw from the wealth of the past and set new trends for the future.

The Keyboard: Today's piano is similar to that of the Romantic period. The invention of synthesizers and digital keyboards has given new sounds for composers to explore.

TABLE OF CONTENTS

FF1030

BAROQUE
1600 - 1750

Canario

Joachim Von der Hofe
(17th century, dates unknown)

Allegretto

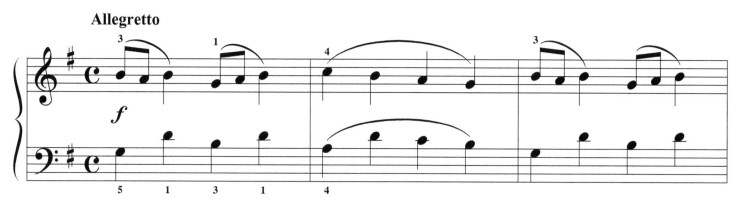

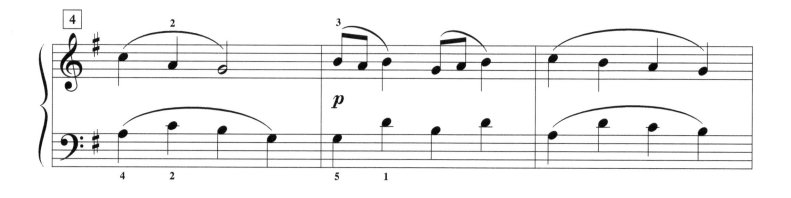

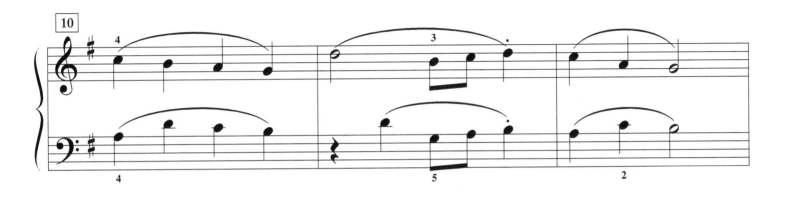

FF1030

Procession in G

Michael Praetorius
(1571–1621)

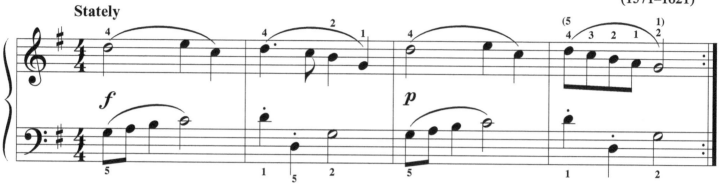

Gavotte in C

Georg Philipp Telemann
(1681–1767)

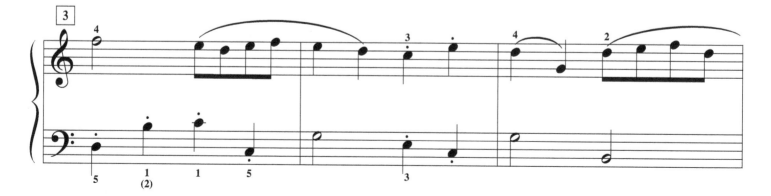

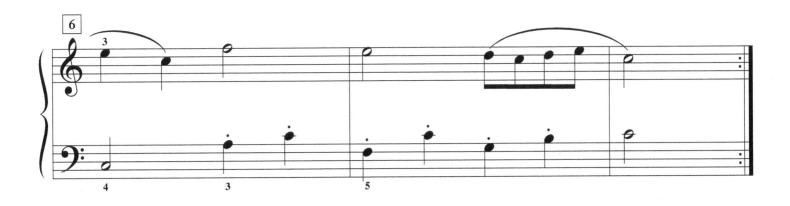

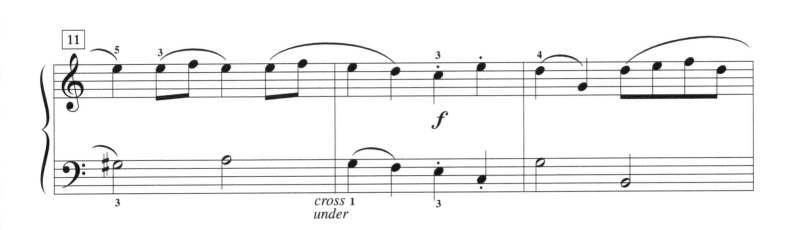

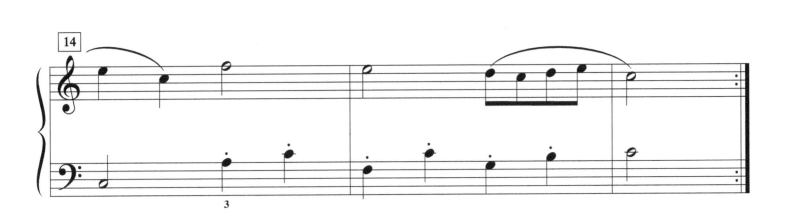

The Highlander
(La Montagnarde)

Jean-Joseph Mouret
(1682–1738)

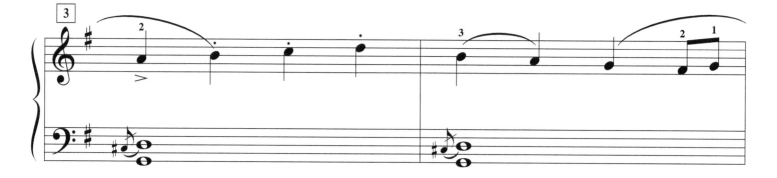

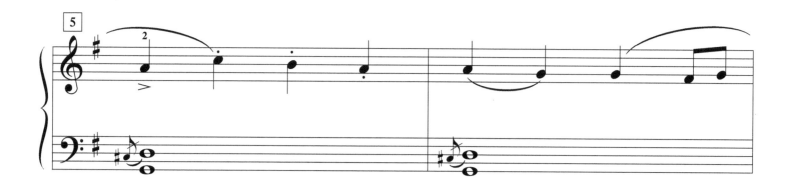

*The student may wish to initially learn this piece without the L.H. grace note.

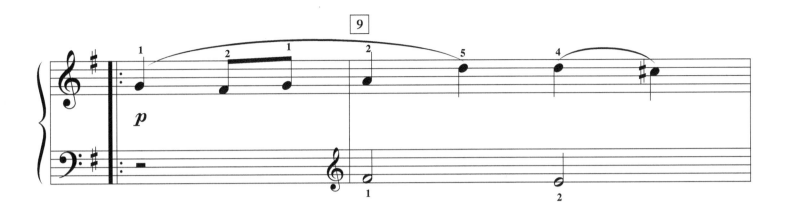

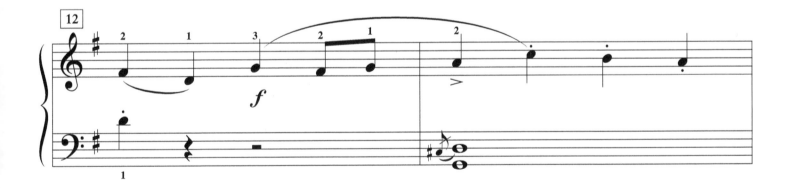

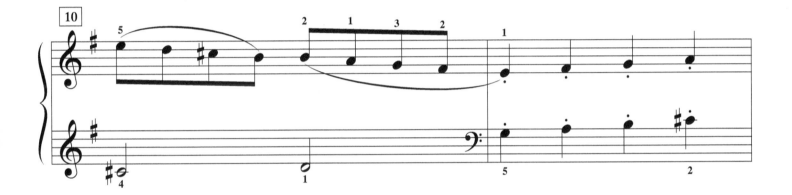

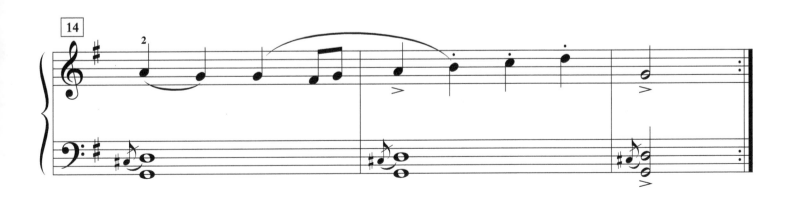

CLASSICAL
1750 - circa 1830

Bagatelle

James Hook
(1746–1827)

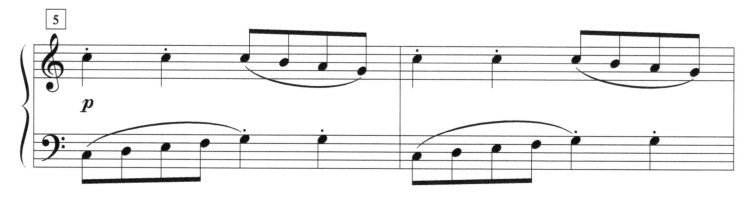

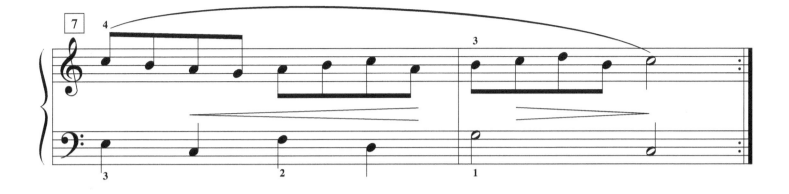

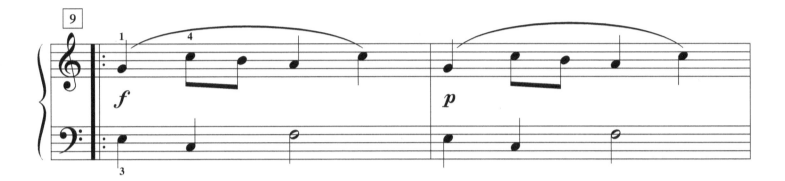

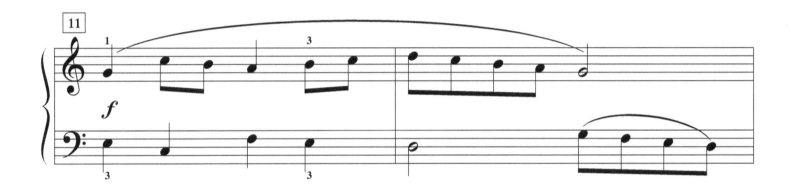

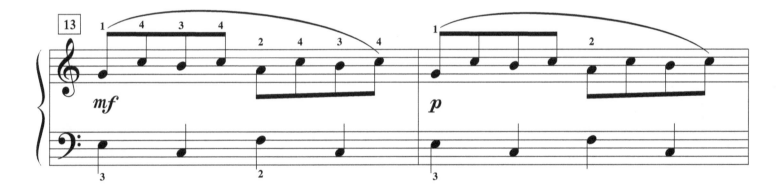

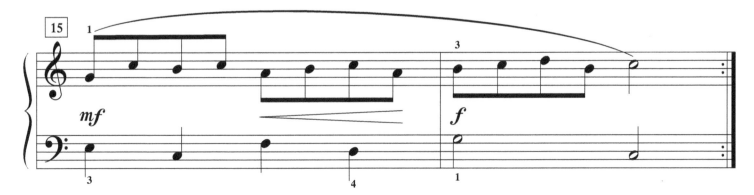

Minuet

James Hook
(1746–1827)

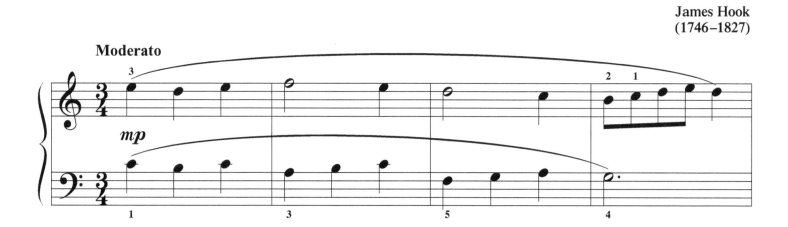

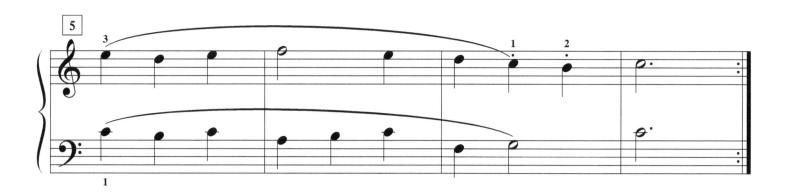

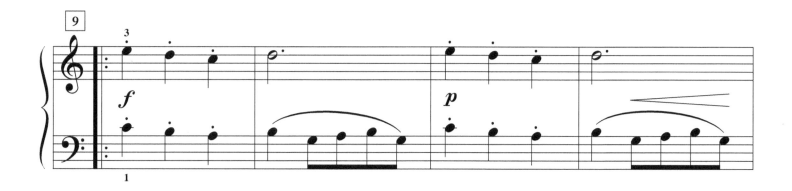

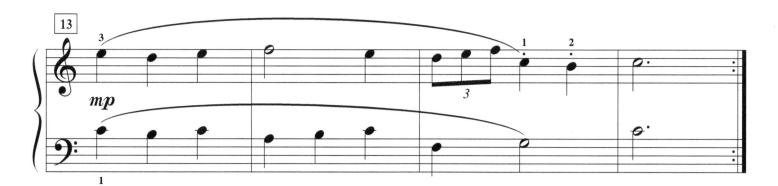

Little Dance

Daniel Gottlob Türk
(1750–1813)

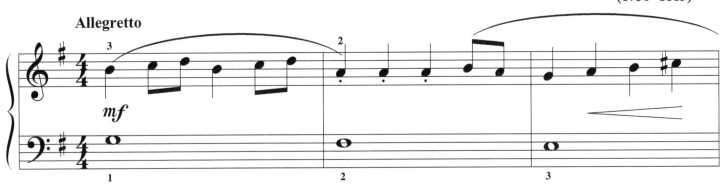

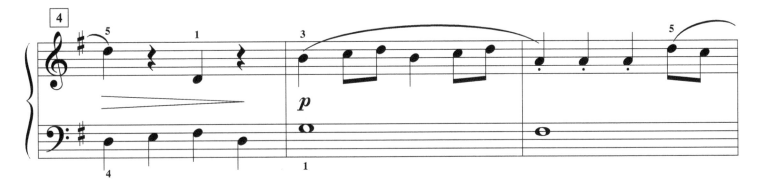

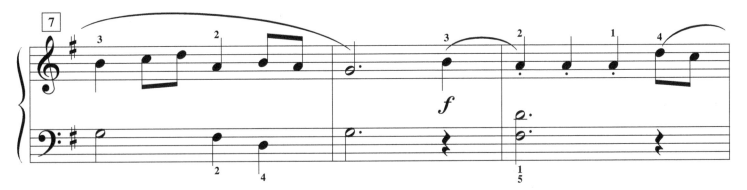

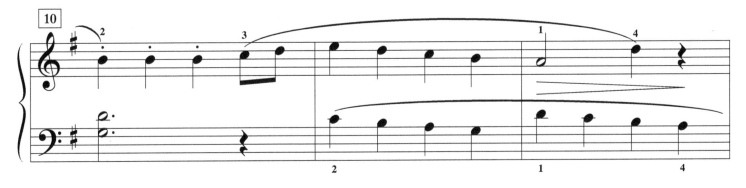

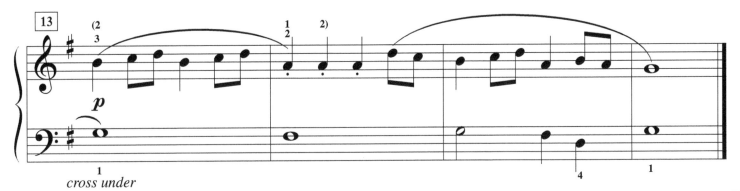

cross under

Morning

Anton Diabelli
(1781–1858)

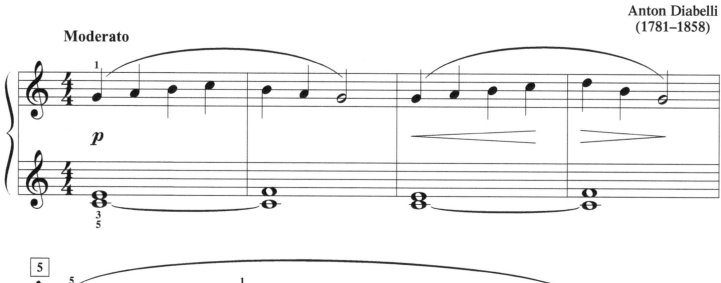

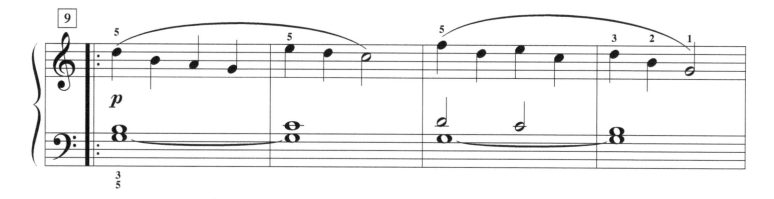

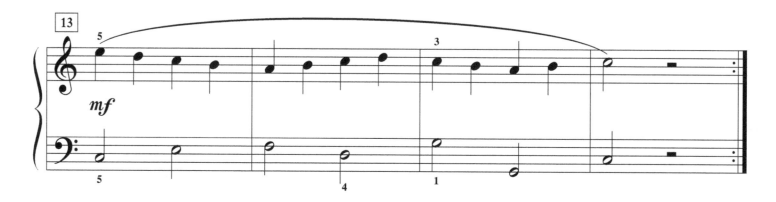

Quadrille

Franz Joseph Haydn
(1732–1809)

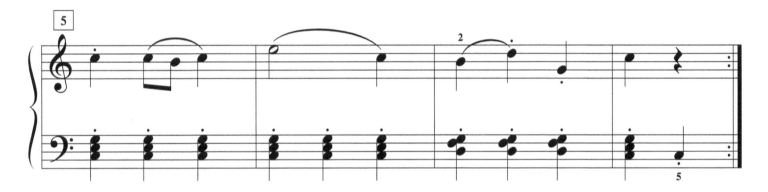

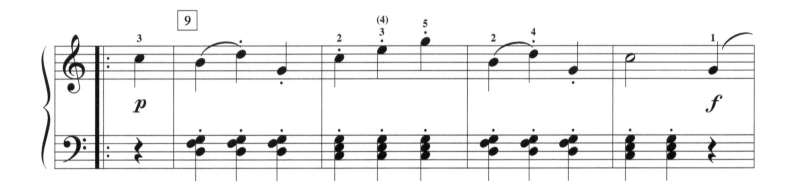

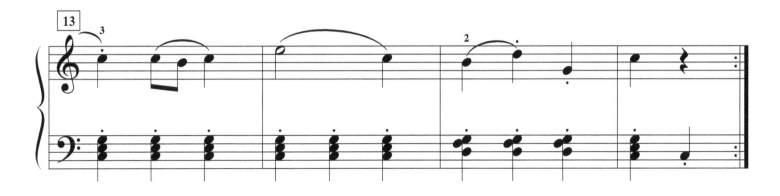

Sonatina in G
(1st movement)

Thomas Attwood
(1765–1838)

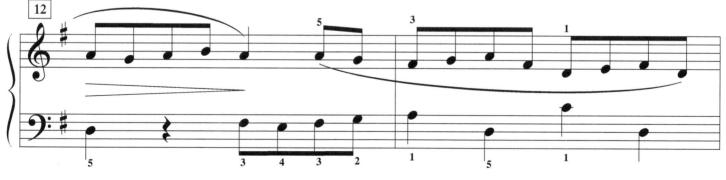

*The slur notation indicates that the D (downbeat of measure 5)
both ends the preceding phrase and begins the new phrase.

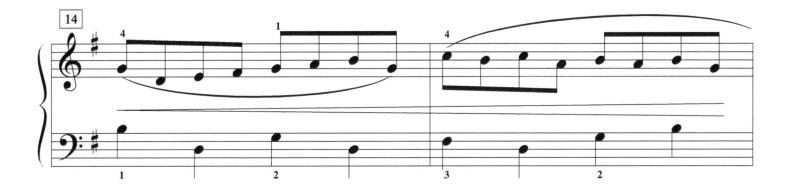

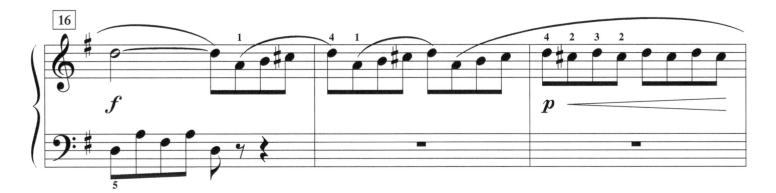

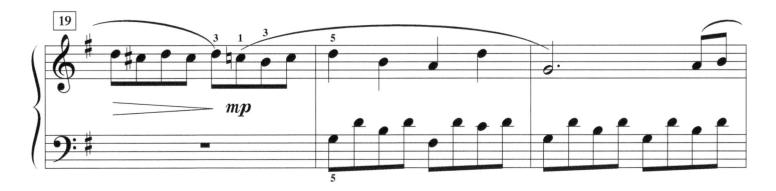

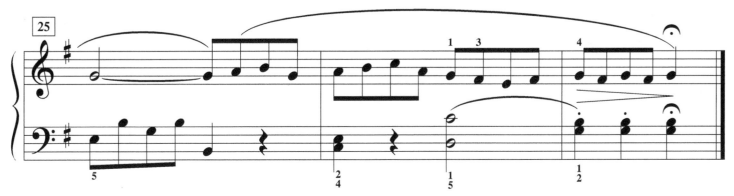

Adagio and Allegro

J.C. Bach and F.P. Ricci
(1735–1782) and (1732–1817)

The *allegro* section may be played freely, as in a *cadenza*.
(A *cadenza* is an elaborate, showy section, often without bar lines.)

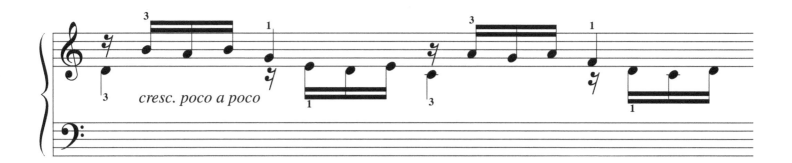

cresc. poco a poco

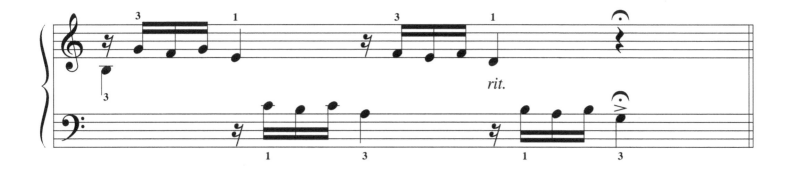

rit.

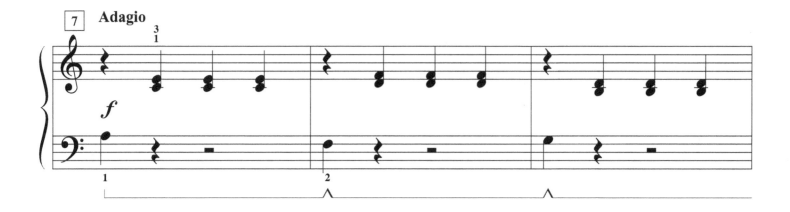

7 **Adagio**

f

10

R.H. over

rit.

ff

Little Prelude

Ludwig Schytte
(1848–1909)

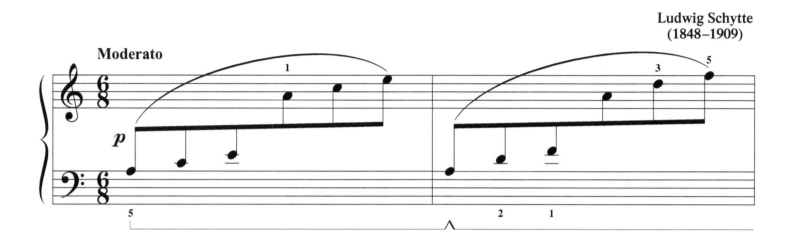

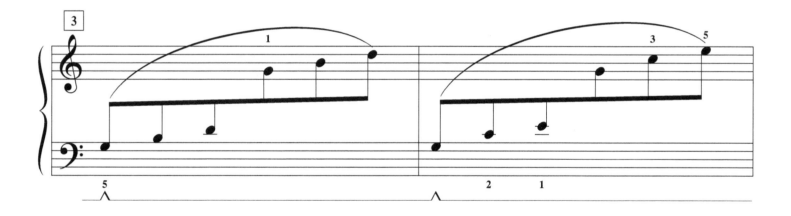

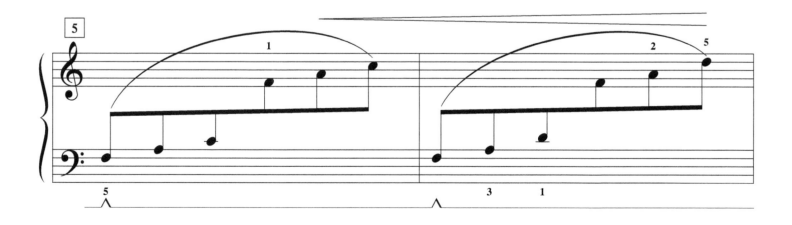

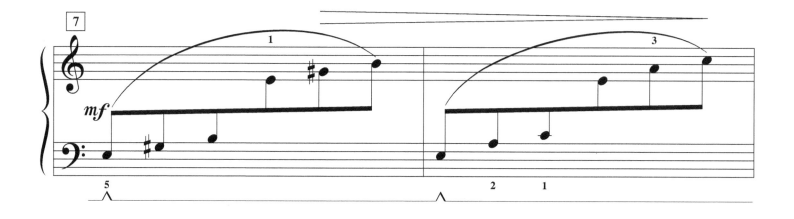

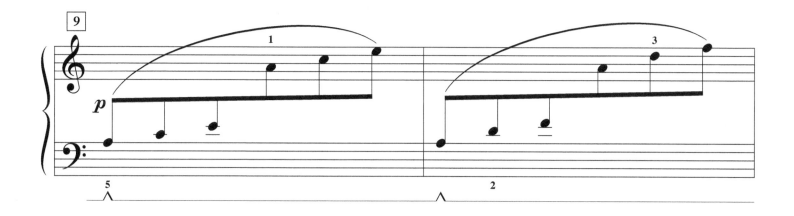

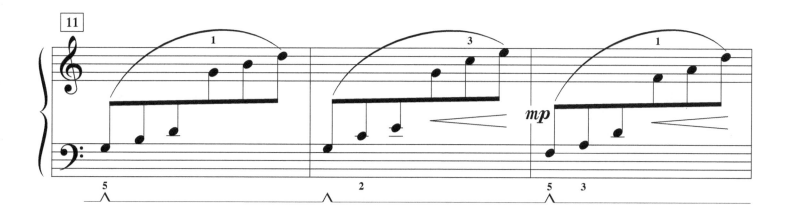

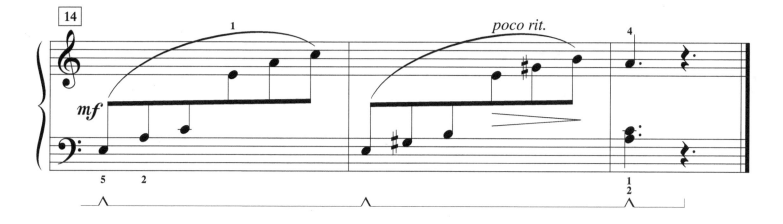

Melody for Left Hand
(Opus 108, No. 12)

Ludwig Schytte
(1848–1909)

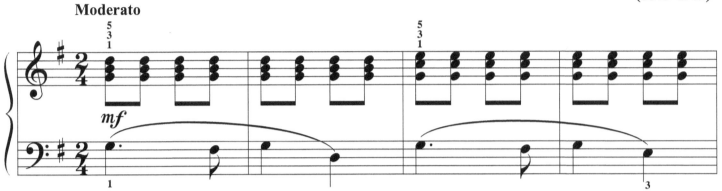

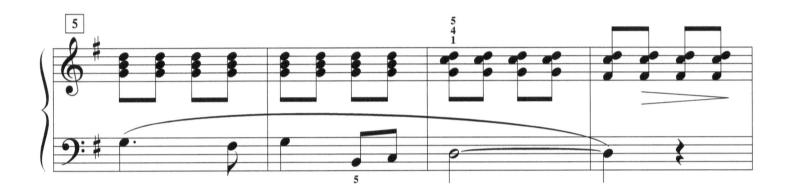

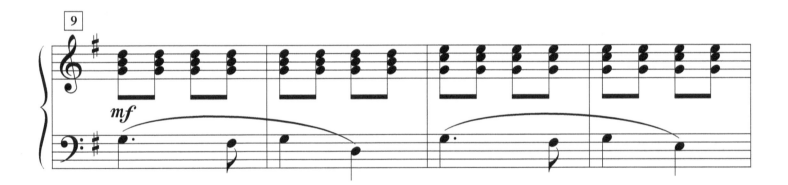

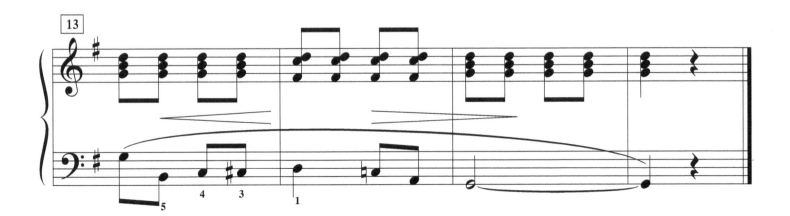

Two Preludes

I

Fritz Spindler
(1817–1905)

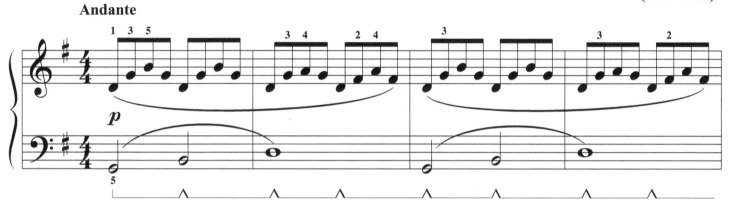

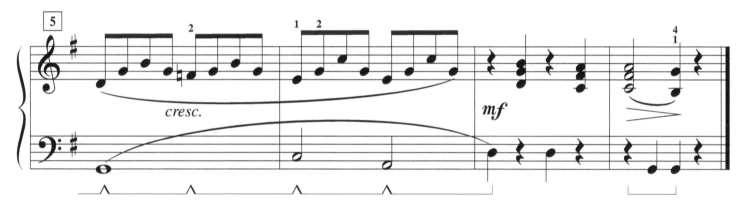

II

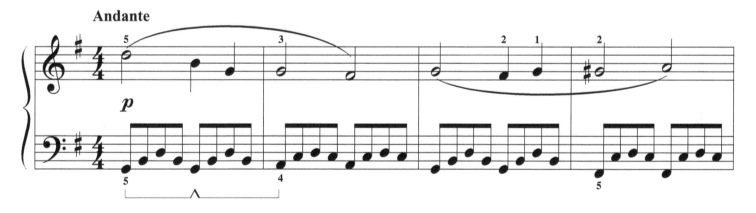

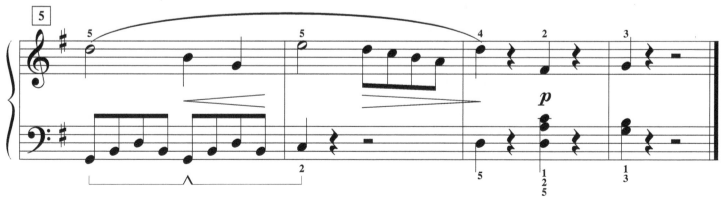

Teacher Part

Waltz for Four Hands
from *The Children's Musical Friend*
(Opus 87, No. 35)

Secondo

Heinrich Wohlfahrt
(1797–1883)

Student Part

Waltz for Four Hands
from *The Children's Musical Friend*
(Opus 87, No. 35)

Primo

Heinrich Wohlfahrt
(1797–1883)

Play BOTH HANDS 1 octave HIGHER throughout.

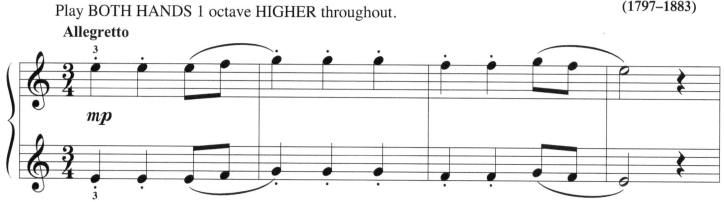

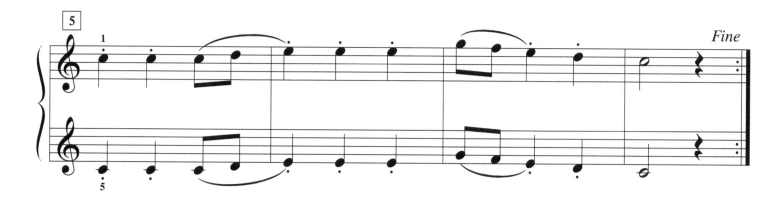

FF1030

The Hunt
(Opus 117, No. 15)

Cornelius Gurlitt
(1820–1901)

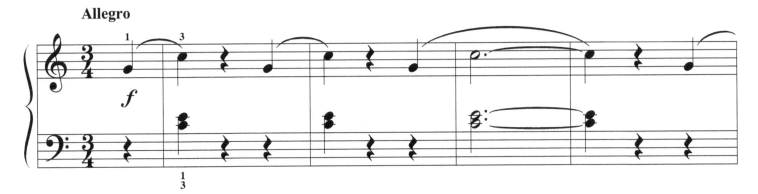

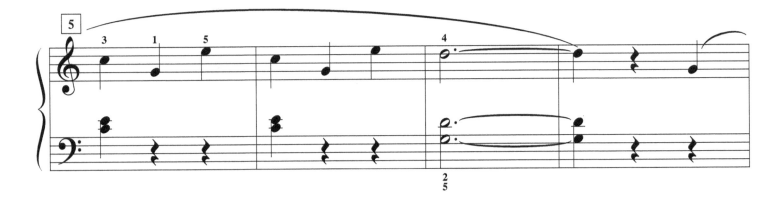

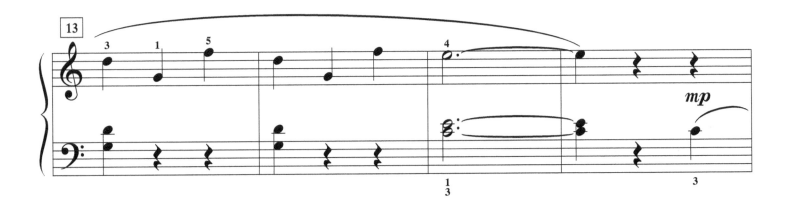

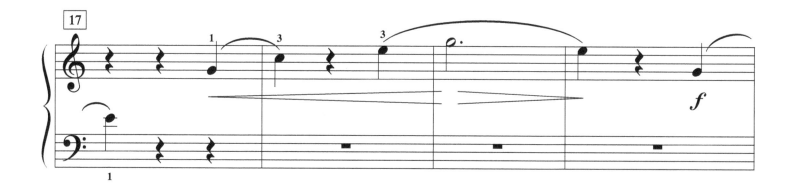

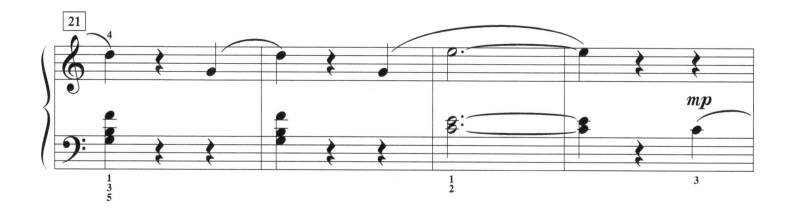

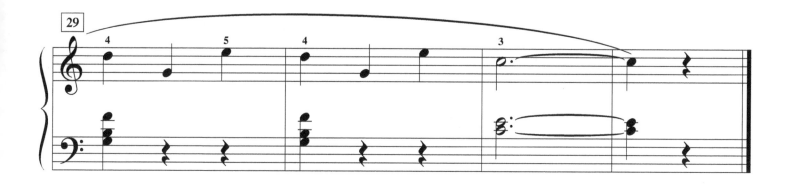

Tarantella
(Opus 14, No. 8)

Frank Lynes
(1858–1913)

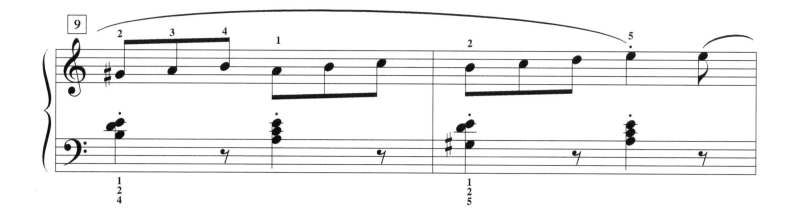

Contemporary
circa 1900–present

On the Ocean Floor
from *The Ocean (Deep Sea Explorations on the Piano)*

Hansi Alt
(20th century, dates unknown)

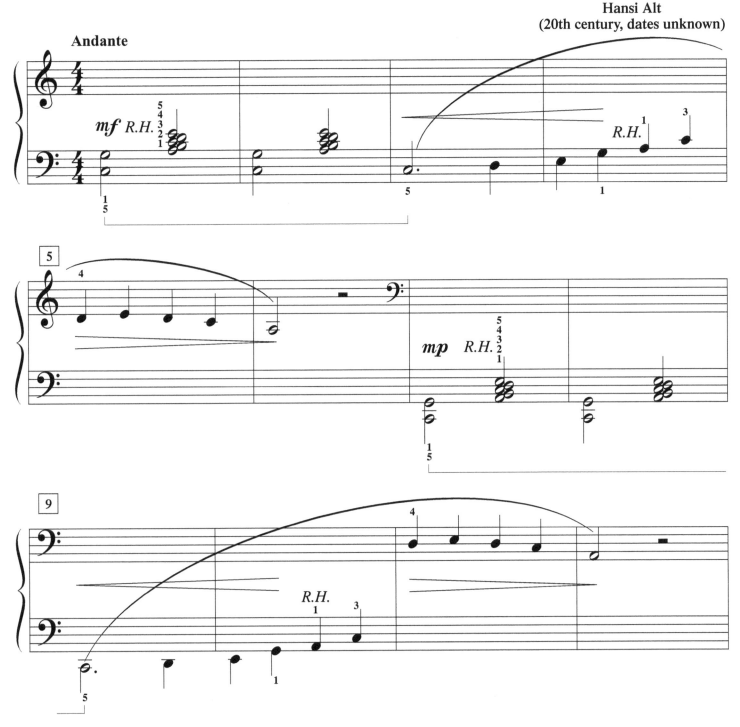

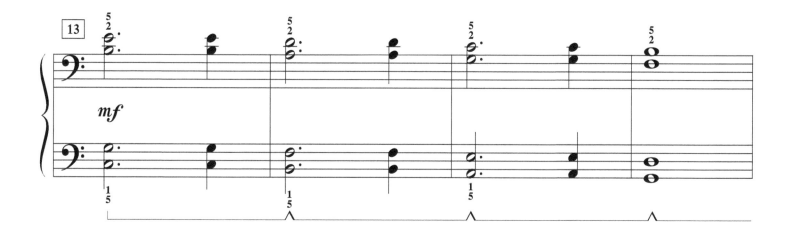

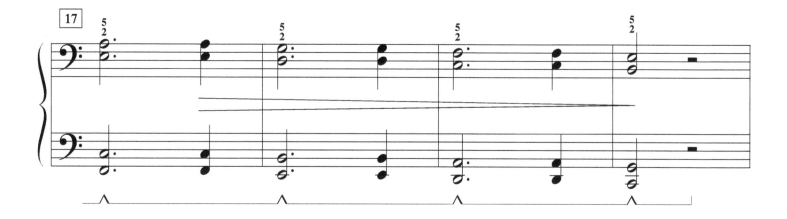

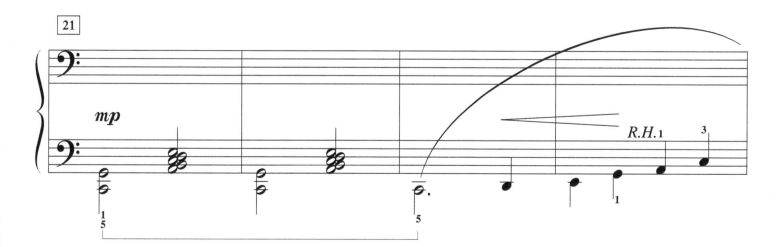

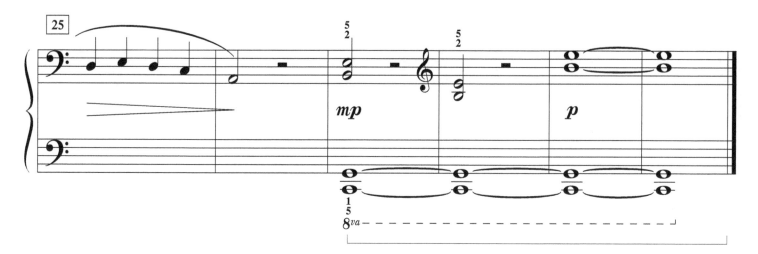

The Busy Machine

V. Dubliansky
(20th century, dates unknown)

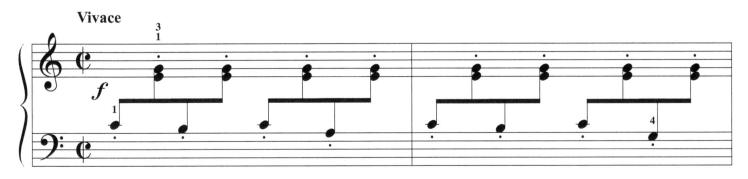

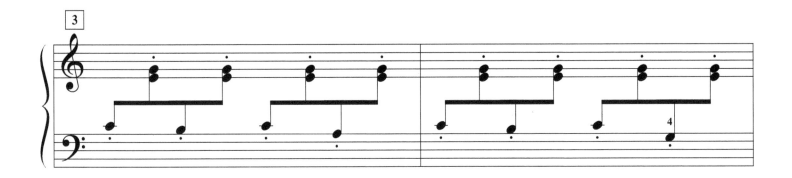

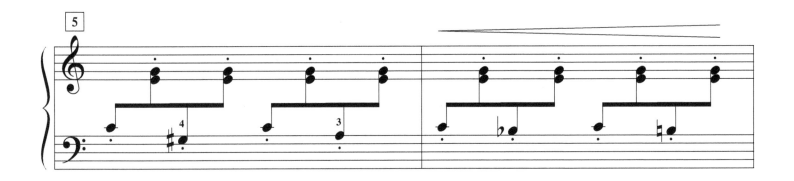

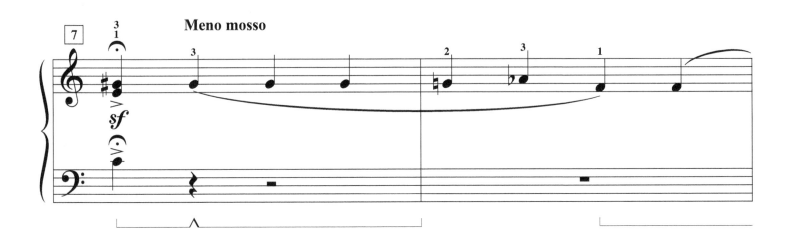

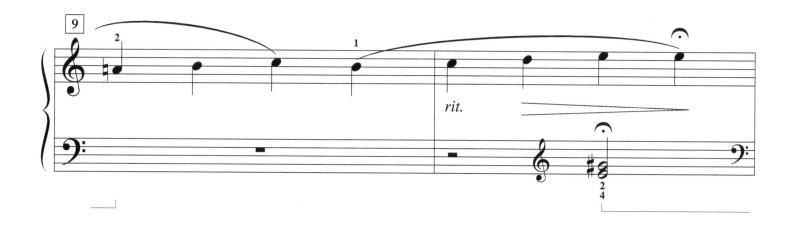

Tempo I

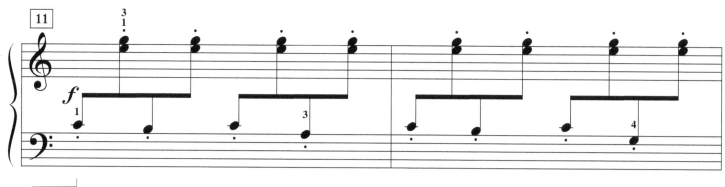

Shepherd Pipes

Tat'iana Salutrinskaya
(Dates unknown)

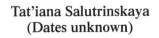

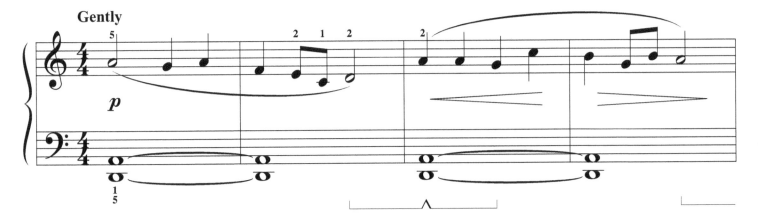

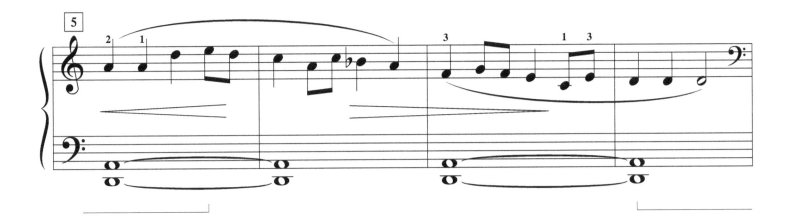

Pantomime

Nancy Faber
(1955–)

Quickly, playfully

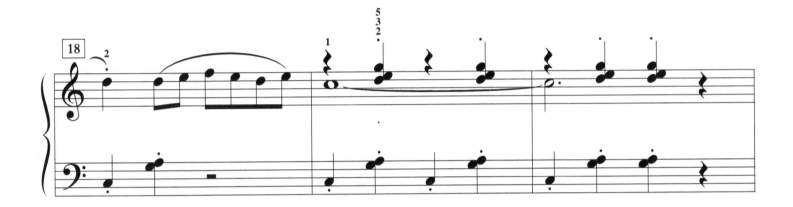

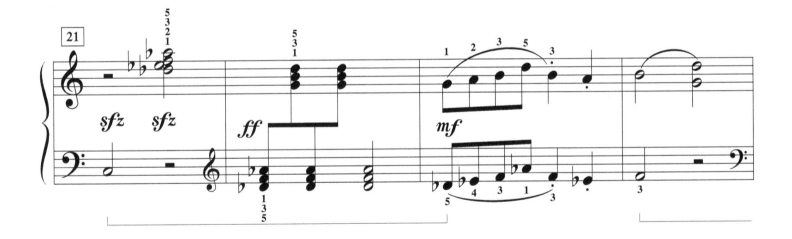

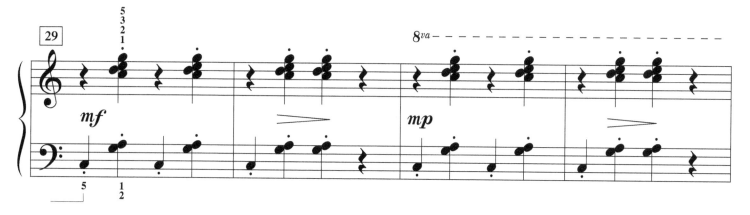

DICTIONARY OF MUSICAL TERMS

DYNAMIC MARKS

pp	*p*	*mp*	*mf*	*f*	*ff*
pianissimo	*piano*	*mezzo piano*	*mezzo forte*	*forte*	*fortissimo*
very soft	soft	moderately soft	moderately loud	loud	very loud

crescendo (cresc.)

Play gradually louder.

diminuendo (dim.) or decrescendo (decresc.)

Play gradually softer.

TEMPO MARKS

Adagio	*Andante*	*Moderato*	*Allegretto*	*Allegro*	*Vivace*
slowly	"walking speed" (slower than *Moderato*)	moderate tempo	rather fast	fast and lively	very fast

SIGN	TERM	DEFINITION
	a tempo	Return to the beginning tempo (speed).
accel.	*accelerando*	Gradually play faster.
	accent	Play this note louder.
	Alberti bass	A left-hand accompaniment that outlines the notes of a chord using the pattern: bottom-top-middle-top.
	bagatelle	A short musical piece, usually written for the piano. Bagatelle literally means "a trifle."
	canario	An old dance that originated in the Canary Islands. The canario was popular in Europe during the Baroque period.
C	**common time**	$\frac{4}{4}$ time. The ♩ gets one beat. Four beats per measure.
¢	**cut time (*alla breve*)**	$\frac{2}{2}$ time. The ♩ gets one beat. Two half-note beats per measure.
⌢	*fermata*	Hold this note longer than usual.
	gavotte	An old French dance in $\frac{4}{4}$ time, beginning with two upbeats. The gavotte is more lively than the minuet.
	grace note	An ornamental note that is played quickly into the note that follows.
	legato	Smoothly; connected.
	meno mosso	Less motion; a little slower.

	minuet	A stately dance in $\frac{3}{4}$ time.
Op.	**opus**	A creative work. A composer's pieces are often numbered in the order in which they were written. Each work is given an *opus* number. Several pieces may be included in a single opus. For example, Op. 3, No. 1; Op. 3, No. 2, etc.
$8^{va} - \rceil$	*ottava*	Play one octave higher than written. When $8^{va} - \lrcorner$ is below the staff, play one octave lower than written.
	poco	A little. For example, *poco rit.* means a little *ritard*.
	poco a poco	Little by little.
	prelude	A short instrumental piece, often rather free in style. Originally, a prelude was used as an introduction to another piece.
	primo	The treble part in a four-hand piano duet.
	quadrille	An early French dance in which couples formed a square.
rit.	*ritardando*	Gradually slow down.
	secondo	The bass part (second part) in a four-hand piano duet.
sfz	**sforzando**	A sudden, strong accent.
♪	**sixteenth note**	One-half the duration of an eighth note. There are four sixteenths to a quarter note.
♯	**sixteenth rest**	Silence for the duration of a sixteenth note.
⌢	**slur**	Connect the notes within a slur.
	sonatina	A little *sonata*. (A *sonata* is a type of instrumental piece, often with several movements.)
♩.	*staccato*	Play notes marked *staccato* detached, disconnected.
	tarantella	A rapid $\frac{6}{8}$ composition. In folklore, the tarantella dance was said to cure the poisonous bite of the tarantula spider.
	tempo	The speed of the music.
	Tempo I	Play at the first *tempo* (speed) of the piece.
♩	**tenuto mark (stress mark)**	Hold this note its full value. Stress the note by pressing gently into the key.
♪♪♪	**triplet**	Three eighth notes equal a quarter note.
	waltz	A waltz is a dance in $\frac{3}{4}$ time.

ALPHABETICAL INDEX OF TITLES

Access audio online at
pianoadventures.com/lit1
password: **zruxp8**

For technical support, visit
pianoadventures.com/contact